Mister Zippy's Adventures In Paradise

By Cindy Fessman

To Don & Bailey

My love, always

Many thanks to Dr. Warshal and the staff at Cooper.

I could not have done this without you.

Foreword

I started writing "Adventures in Paradise" as a way of staying in touch with our friends and family in the States. Don and I had sold our respective businesses, and we began to ponder the question, "Where do we really want to live?" Did we want to live near the kids and grandchildren? They were all spread from Los Angeles to Tampa to Denver to Charlotte. Any of those cities would offer us a nice lifestyle, but what was the guarantee they wouldn't move away from us at some point?

Without giving the question much thought, I opened my big mouth and the words just slid out easily, "On an island. Let's live on an island." So we put together a business plan to run catamaran day trips out of St. Croix, thinking we needed to be in U.S. territory. We had friends in St. Croix that we had visited earlier in the year, and we decided it could be a terrific place to live.

Within five days, we realized this was not the island, not the business, not the time; none of the above. "Let's go to St. Maarten. We've always loved it there!" I exclaimed. So here we were, several days later, post 9-11, buying a three-bedroom, three-bath villa with a pool, in a gated community on the ocean in Dutch St. Maarten, where we could enjoy nice neighbors, fantastic sunsets, and the continual glow of a glorious tan. The bonus of all this was to awaken each day to the sound of gentle waves breaking on the coral rocks below. We moved there to Sunset Villa months later, in May 2002.

For the first two years, we spent eight to nine months of the year in St. Maarten and the remainder of our time in Avalon, New Jersey, also known as the "Jersey Shore." It was a great life.

I had not felt well for about six months, and in September, 2005, a doctor in St. Maarten diagnosed my advanced-stage ovarian cancer. Although it was difficult to leave our "new" home in St. Maarten, we returned to the States immediately for medical care. We were referred to an excellent gynecological oncologist surgeon, who went right to work on me taking the bad stuff out of my body. My chemotherapy began six weeks later. In all the years since that time, I alternated with chemo and remission in twelve-month intervals. During the intervals of chemo, we made every effort to return to St. Maarten after treatment, because the climate was so restorative – to all three of us.

Having been engaged in my fight with ovarian cancer for three years now, I can honestly say that a certain inner beauty can arise after a valiant battle with cancer. I feel it and I see it in myself. Even in times of pain and discomfort, I can tell you it has been years since I have felt or looked as healthy as I do now.

So, through the loving care of my husband, Don, the unwavering loyalty of Bailey One and Bailey Two (Mister Zippy), and the unwavering support of our family and friends, I have emerged stronger and leaner, and with a wisdom and beauty like never before, much like a butterfly emerging from its cocoon.

I send a million thank you's to Mike, Kelly & Jim, Keira & Connor, Lisa & Dave, Cole, Sammy, and Don II. We could not have gotten through this without your love and dedication.

Now, I'd like to share with you the antics of Mister Zippy and our Adventures in Paradise, from his point of view.

Enjoy!

Bailey on the terrace

Chapter One

The New "Me"

Hello, Everybody –

I am a golden retriever, three and a half months old. My name is Bailey Junior, but they call me "Mister Zippy" because I can spin around really, really fast.

It distresses me to admit that I am a replacement pet for Bailey One, who died two days ago! You see, Bailey got very sick and the doctors had to rule out viruses, bacteria, and parasites and all that bad stuff and they finally found a mass in his liver, and it spread to other organs but it was too late to do anything about it. Mom Cindy made him all kinds of good stuff to coax him to eat – scrambled eggs, sautéed liver, and grilled cheese, while Daddy Don brought him his favorite double cheeseburgers with ketchup only and French fries on the side. Yum. I wish they'd do that for me...

Mom & Dad were pretty heartsick when they lost Bailey, and here I was – sitting in the same pet store, AND in the same kennel where Bailey One first found Mom! It was one of Dad's pet stores he used to own, in Newark, Delaware. Again, they tell me it was "love at first sight". Mom had a big smile and I love the way she held me and petted me and loved on me... She really wanted to take me home with her. Mom later told me that Dad was a "Man on a Mission" to find the right "Me". Boy, I am sure one happy pup! I love them both.

I really want them to love me for myself, but the understanding is that I have very big shoes to fill. They say I look like I could be Bailey's little boy. I am the same, beautiful dark reddish-brown color, but I am pretty little, and I have a white blaze above my nose.

I love to live with Mom & Dad, but I am confused about <u>where</u> we live. I thought it was Avalon, NJ, and we had a nice routine established there, but now we are in St. Maarten, somewhere in the Caribbean and everything is very different – but nice. I am sure one happy pup!

I was really happy to come to St. Maarten on the airplane. The experience of getting here was half the fun. Mom and Dad choose really big planes to fly on, mainly for my safety and comfort. They also fly "direct" which means we don't have to change planes in Puerto Rico or Miami, and run the risk of losing baggage or, Heaven forbid, losing ME! They put my crate underneath with the food. The air is temperature controlled, and the flight crew can visit whenever they want. I really like the ladies in the flight crews because they O-o-o and Ah-h-h over me all the time! It is cool for me down there, too. I was wonderfully good on the trip. I got so much attention, I forgot to bark. Much.

We all learned right away on how important our manners are in St. Maarten. For me, I was told to just sit at attention and be quiet. For Mom and Dad, whoever they come into contact with, whether it is a stranger they pass on the street, in a store, in a restaurant, when they ask directions, etc. or when they see a neighbor or a friend or a workman, they should first and foremost say "Good Morning" or "Good Afternoon". Nothing else a person may have on their minds is as important as these two words. If Mom or Dad asks their question or makes their request BEFORE they extend this greeting, then the other person will look at them as though they are from another planet, because as far as they are concerned, Mom and Dad are! Other good manners include wishing your friend a "Good Day". My favorite of all time is the double air kiss on both cheeks, (French version) and the triple air kiss (Dutch version). I really sit at attention for these treats!

Driving on our island is an art and a science that can best be described as a "merge society". Once I saw a red pickup truck pass us, but it was all wrong. He was going backward! We observed there are few to no traffic lights on the island. Instead, there are lots of traffic circles and T-intersections. Dad says we have to be patient and allow others the right of way. When you do use your horn, Mom discovered that one short blast is the greeting for a woman while two short blasts are for a guy. A longer blast means, "Get the hell out of my way, I'm a comin' through."

Every day, I get to take swimming lessons in our own swimming pool. The water is nice and warm and clean, not soapy like a bath. The first step has about an inch of water on it, which is fine. But, boy, the second step is a killer. Well, it is a <u>whole</u> step down, which is a really long way for me because I'm so little! I keep putting my head under water to look for the step, and I paw at it, too. It's a strange experience. There's a big feeling I have where I think I should be swimming, since I AM a golden retriever. They call it an "instink". So every once in a while, I can "launch" myself and there I go; I swim out a little bit and then swim back. It's fun but really scary, because there's nothing underneath me but water. The second time I did this, I turned the corner and went left in the pool – I felt a momentary panic because it was big open water, and my little legs were getting real tired before I figured out where to go to save myself ... The steps. I needed to find the steps!

They have little iguanas here in St. Maarten – lizards, actually, and they are called geckos. I love these little guys and they are so fun to chase. (I wonder what they taste like?) I see them all the time when Mom and Dad take me outside - about every hour. I guess they think I need the exercise, but it is really part of our "roo-teen".

There's one little gecko buddy who comes out to the edge of the front yard to greet us every morning. He has a split tail, so Dad named him "Sparky", because he looks like he should plug in somewhere. No kidding! Anyway, we started bringing Sparky a blueberry every morning. He'd smile up at us, pick up his blueberry, and run off to his little home between the rocks by the house. I think he likes us. I also wonder if his little gecko family is like ours – warm and fun and huggy, too.

The other thing they have here in St. Maarten is lots and lots of toys to play with; I "inherited" them from Bailey One. There's Purple Puppy, and Foxy, Spot, Blue Doggy, Yellow Doggy, Baby Kitty, Little Puppy, Monkey, and Ducky. Oh yes, I could go on and on. It'll take me a lifetime to learn who everybody is, so that when Dad asks me to fetch Purple Puppy, I'll know which one to pick up to bring to him. Meanwhile, Mom has a hissy fit almost every day. She says she has to pick up FIVE

THOUSAND toys a day! Boy, that sounds like a lot of toys to me, and I don't even have five thousand toys. I know I just love to put them in my mouth, as many as I can fit at one time, which may be two or three. I run through the house and I zip around and I toss them over my head and side-to-side, and they go EVERYWHERE! Mom just puts her hands on her hips and she shakes her head. Maybe she needs some animal toys, too!

Yesterday, I took Ducky out for a swim, but he just can't get the hang of it. He's drying out in the laundry room right now. Even though he can't swim, luckily, he can still quack.

Right now, I am supposed to be asleep. They said I was getting cranky and needed a nap. Dad took me to Mullet Bay this morning to run and play in the water, while Mom rested in bed for a little while. You see, she is sick with Cancer and gets tired a lot, and she has to have chemo treatments every month for a year! That's a lot. Meanwhile, it was scary to me in the ocean because of the big waves. They went right over me, and tumbled me around! I'm sure glad we don't have those wave things here in our pool.

In a little while, I will get another swimming lesson, and maybe Ducky can try again, too! We'll both practice some more.

Well, let me finish my rest and I will write again soon when I have more adventures to share with you.

All the best,

Bailey Junior / Mister Zippy

Bailey swimming in the water, Mullet Bay

Chapter Two

Fun at the Beach

Hi again, everybody –

I am now almost four months old, which means I am really growing up fast! Mom and Dad tell me in about two months time, they will take me to the Dog Hospital to be "tutored". They read in the Philadelphia papers that if I am embarrassed after I'm neutered, they will consider getting me some neutical implants so's I can be a real, regular guy. Just think about it. Cool, huh!

I finally got my second big day on the beach, ever! It was Orient Bay, which they say is one of the most beautiful beaches in the world. I think it is, too, because it has such sugary sand, and clear water, and petite, cute French girls who run around "topless" on the beach. I had a blast! Mom said I shoulda been a termite because I dug this humongous hole between their chairs. She said it was like an LA freeway interchange, and her chair was ready to collapse. Twenty-two inches deep, yessiree! I really liked crawling under the chairs and digging like that. Never did it before.

I still don't like those wave things in the water but they are pretty little at Orient Beach, and I can swim pretty well now. Dad said he doesn't want to take the leash off me yet, because I might swim off into the sunset. I also like to visit the pretty

French girls on the beach, too. I wag my tail and I sit and they tell me how sweet I am. Oh, and I am learning French words, too, like "A-say-ay-voo", which means, "Please sit down", and "Ah-ten-see-own", which I think is "Please listen to me," which is not easy for me to do...

Anyway, I got so-o-o tired on the beach and I tried to take a nap, but Dad kept waking me up to make sure I was OK. You see, I chewed up a bug trap this morning and they could only find about half of the chewed up pieces. Dad was worried the bug killer medicine would make me sick and sleepy, but the digging and swimming was what really made me sleepy. All I wanted to do was snooze under the chair, but he decided he should keep me awake the whole time! He finally walked me way over to the side where the grass and bushes are located so I could potty, and boy – once I saw the grass, I really woke up. I rolled and flipped around in the grass and then he knew I was OK! I guess I sure had him fooled. Oh, and we are starting to find the little black chewed up pieces, but I won't tell you where...

The only time I need to bark these days is at five in the morning to see if I can get Dad up. Yup. I'm getting him trained in his "roo-teen", too. He comes out of the bedroom and lets me out of my kennel and I sit for him (A-say-ay-voo). He puts my collar and leash on, and we go out, starting our walk, as usual, with a blueberry for Sparky. The best part is – after our walk, I trained Dad to let me go swim a few laps in the pool! This way, I get a good rubdown with the towel and I am now ready for a serious Hungry Boy breakfast.

Today, I couldn't wake Mom 'n Dad up until ten after six, so I barked and yes, you guessed it – Dad got up and we went out for our morning "roo-teen". Now I am so-o-o tired, I need to take a nap again and I am too tired to write anymore. So let me rest for an hour or two with Mom, and then I will be back on the computer to say "Hi" to you again.

Please stay as sweet as you are, and always remember – I prefer the small-sized biscuits, thank you very much.

Oh, and Ducky still can't swim. I think we are giving up on that idea.

Love and biscuits,

Mister Zippy

Gallion Bay Beach

Chapter Three

My Girlfriend

Hi again, everybody –

I am so happy to tell you – I HAVE A GIRLFRIEND IN ST. MAARTEN! Yes. She's big, black, and beautiful, and she just turned two years old! Her name is Bentley and she's a gorgeous Rottweiler who lives a couple of doors away. We might even be related, I don't know. Her mom Brittany and dad Ryan have adopted my mom and dad, so does that make us cousins or what? See, Bentley's mom is a student at the medical school, and they always invite my mom and dad when they need parents here and they go to parties together, too.

The nicest thing about having a girlfriend is that I haven't yet developed "bad habits" - except I tinkle a little on people's feet when they come over to visit. Especially women. I get excited when they O-o-o and Ah-h-h over me.

I really like to take Bentley swimming with me, but she just can't get the hang of it. She sinks in the pool and everybody gets upset when this happens. Me? I just glide around in the water like it is effortless. Simple, actually. After all, I **am** a retriever. Don't know yet if Bentley knows how to dig tunnels under the chairs at the beach… I may have to show her how to do that, too.

I find it interesting that Mom doesn't call me Mister Zippy anymore – now she refers to me as "Wild Child". I can still zip around, but boy I can get pretty wild, too. You should see how fast I can go from one end of the house to the other, and back and forth and back and forth... I need to have Dad time me; I'm that good!

Tomorrow is my big day to be neutered at the vet. I am now five and a half months old and Mom says that'll fix my wagon, but good! I'm supposed to be ready about six o'clock in the afternoon. Does that mean they are taking me out to dinner, too? After they tutor me, I think I get to just lie around for a while and rest.

Mom has a good doctor she found in Marigot, a beautiful French town that is the capital of French St. Martin. We live on the Dutch side. The doctor specializes in treating cancer patients and survivors, like Mom, and he does acupuncture, nutrition, and treats metabolic diseases. He gave Mom a great deep-tissue massage and stuck some acupuncture needles in her when she wasn't looking. She probably looked a little like a porcupine, don't you think? The doctor wants to do this every week, and he also put her on a special diet, which I have to tell you about. The diet is a riot. No wheat, no dairy, no soy, no corn. She can have rice milk instead of milk, which I think tastes pretty good... She drinks the juice from three lemons every morning and every evening. Every Monday and Thursday, she eats a quarter of a fresh pineapple every two hours, then a large green salad at 7 p.m. Otherwise, she can have vegetables, fruits, rice stuff, other grains, beans, seafood, chicken and a steak once in a while. Funny, she says the lemon juice takes away her taste for wine, so we don't see her drinking wine or anything – supposedly a wine spritzer when they go out, but I don't think she enjoys that very much, really.

Dad says he is doing part of the same diet as Mom, and his running has improved immensely. He is a marathon runner with sixty-five marathons under his belt. Twenty-three were prestigious Boston Marathons. Last weekend, he took third place in a Bastille Day race in Marigot – for age group fifty to ninety-nine! Way-to-go, Dad!!

Oh, guess what… Mom says her cancer has returned, so we are going up to the States next week to get her "fixed". She is feeling tired and rundown, but that's where I come in. You see, when I rest with her, Mom tells me about her cancer and what the treatments are like and how she feels, where it hurts, what she needs to do, and the medicines to take, and special foods to eat to keep her feeling good. Helping her is a lot of work for me, but I love her dearly and she can talk to me about anything. That's my JOB!

Returning to the States means that some of you might get to meet me sooner than later. But give us a week or two. I guarantee we will be running around in circles until we get ourselves settled.

I look forward to seeing you soon. I think you'll like me. I'm a cutie!

Love and biscuits,

Mister Zippy

Bailey in raft with Mom

Chapter Four

I Get "Tutored"

Hi again, everybody –

We are back in the States for medical reasons again, finishing up our thirty-night stay in a hotel because our house in Avalon, is rented out to summer weekly tenants. Right now, Mom gets chemotherapy every Thursday, and then she has a week off. You'd be real proud of her. She's doing well, except when she's not. You see, the effects of chemo run through her body and it affects everything – skin, digestive tract, appetite, loss of hair, nails, energy level, muscle aches, bone pain, you name it. But remember – that's what I'm here for, to take care of Mom.

One cold, windy afternoon, she tripped and fell in the street. I wanted to go one way and she wanted to go the other, and I pulled her off balance, so she fell. But don't worry. I stood over her to protect her so the cars wouldn't hit her! I wouldn't let them near her. One car finally stopped and the man asked Mom if she needed help with me. Hah! I said, but I don't think he understood. "Yes, please." So he came over and took my leash and led me away. I did not want to go too far, but it was just enough so that Mom could get up off the street. She was crying and all skinned up on her knees and hands. Another person helped her to the sidewalk. When Mom and I were reunited, I realized this was serious, and I needed to take better care of her! So I did. I took her home and we went to bed - my favorite place in the whole world!

When we finally got our house in Avalon back, it was right in the middle of our whole-house re-carpeting project! The tenants were gone and we could take our time putting personal stuff back into place, like we lived there. We expect to be here until Mom finishes this round of chemo, about six months, during which time we plan to take a few short trips to St. Maarten.

Mom is doing very well. Chemo is fairly easy this time, and not as toxic as before. She says she's experienced little to no side effects, and she gets to keep her hair and fingernails! On chemo day, they start her drip and as soon as it hits her system, she is out cold until it's time to leave, usually around noon. Easy. Dad drives us home and Mom continues to sleep it off. Then she gets some real bursts of energy and starts all kinds of projects with the help of a little steroid that soups her up. She even looks pretty normal... usually.

For me, I am almost seven months old, and let's be clear; I am a real brat now. I'm so good, I can locate a chicken bone or a dead gecko a half-mile away, and pop it into my mouth before Mom or Dad can catch me. Truly. And I'm handsome, too. Mom 'n Dad are doing a LOT of manners training with me. Yessireebob! Mom, unfortunately, doesn't have a lot of patience right now, and Dad, well, he has to do the training with me over and over and over and over... It's not that I forget; it's just that maybe I don't wanna do what they want me to do.

It was real easy getting neutered last month. Just a simple "snip" and they were done. But when Dad and Mom first took me in for my neuter appointment, they were making fun with the guy at the desk and told him to make sure the doc implanted "Neuticals" into my "empty spaces". The guy told us, "Don't laugh. We had a dog owner who made a special trip to the States just to buy a pair of Neutical implants for his male dog. Reason being, they didn't want the dog to be embarrassed that he was "missing" something. Well, the doc implanted the Neuticals and everything went well except when the dog woke up and started running around, they realized the Neuticals were one size too big!" Is this possible? I don't want to hear your answer...

I hope to see **you** soon. Love and biscuits to all of you -

Mister Zippy

Don & Bailey in foyer

Chapter Five

Avalon Adventures

Hi again, everybody –

We are enjoying our time in Avalon. Dad works with me every day with the training collar and sometimes with a leash. We practice manners, obedience, and all the do's and don'ts of puppyhood, like not running across the street, and things like that. But I get confused when cars slow down when they see me. I always think they are coming over to say "Hi" to me. Same with the workmen across the street. Dad gets really upset when I run over to see them. I know they just want to pet me and say nice things...We are training me very intensely to become a service dog for Mom. I am already her constant companion and I rest on the bed with her and fetch her things. She usually has lots of energy except when she doesn't(!) and then her body says STOP, and she has to rest. That's where I come in...

We had a really scary time one night during our walk. Dad put my training collar on and took me up to the beach on the beach path. He let me off the leash so I could run around in the dunes, and go potty, which I do, frequently. It was 9:30 at night. I heard an animal sound and then I smelled him, so I went over to say "Hi". Oh no… it was a SKUNK!

I have now learned the hard way that skunks are not nice or fun animals. He sprayed me really well, and now I stink to high heaven! I ran back to Dad and he immediately knew what happened and what to do about it. Yes. We ran home, found Mom, and we asked her what to wash me with. Dad wanted to bring me into the bathroom and wash me in the big tub, but Mom is the boss of the bathroom and she told him, "No way, Jose! Here is a big can of tomato sauce and some shampoo and cleaning soap you can try, and lots of towels." So we spent the next hour out on the porch getting washed and shampooed, and scrubbed and cleaned. When Dad finally brought me into the house, I still had some smell, but not as bad as before, certainly. The next day, Dad got some more special soap and scrubbed me again until I was sore. It worked. But somehow, I think a little of the skunk smell will always remain with me.

Mom says I'm becoming quite a nice young man, with manners and good looks, and affection galore. My favorite time is when I rest up on the bed with Mom and keep her company. She really likes that.

I'm growing up so fast! Love to you all!

Mister Zippy

Don, Bailey & Cindy on Terrace

Chapter Six

Rest & Recovery

Hi again, everybody –

It has been a long seven months since I last talked to you. And I sure hope you are not all sitting around worrying about Mom just because you haven't heard from us! In January, they put the big guns on Mom and she couldn't write for me for a long time. These were the best, strongest front-line chemotherapy chemicals for ovarian cancer, and it worked. Yay! Currently, we're here in Paradise, just shy of two weeks, and then we return to the States late next week.

Tomorrow, Mom plans to go with the "girls" on a specially chartered boat over to the island of Tintemarre for the mud baths that occur naturally in the ground. She says you smear it all over your body and then stand in the warm sun to let it dry. When it starts to crackle, you get into the crystal clear water and rub it off. I'm sure Mom's skin will be soft and silky when she gets back. She'll be happy, too.

I grew up a lot during these seven months, and we had a lot more intensive training with manners and such. Since I was spending so much time resting with Mom because she needed me by her side, Dad first made me into an "emotional support service animal". We traveled back to the States every three weeks for treatment and I was able to go with them on the plane and lay at their feet. Cool, huh! But we were met with resistance in some of the airports. We would show all our documentation and doctor letters, but somehow, airport people think dogs, even trained ones on a leash, are going to poop and tinkle and bite somebody. The resistance was difficult, so we took a BIG step, and after a lot of special training, I became an official SERVICE DOG. Yesiree! I have a beautiful black and red vest that says "Service Dog" on the back, and now I just prance through the airport next to Dad, with Mom in a wheelchair with an attendant who takes us to the front of every line.

As a true Service Dog, I am very proud. It is important work, you know, and I take it quite seriously. My vest even has a special tag that says I am allowed ANYWHERE in public areas. People are impressed when they see me, and they frequently ask if they can pet me. When this happens, we have to gracefully tell them, "No, I'm sorry, but he is working." They understand. But part of the truth is that if they did pet me, I might enjoy it so much I'd forget I was working and tinkle unexpectedly on the floor!

During the summer months when we come back for treatment and our "Jersey Shore" house in Avalon is rented by the week, we stay in nice hotels for three or four nights, and then fly back to St. Maarten when the chemo is finished. Dad picks hotels where Service Dogs stay for free. I was nervous in the hotels at first, and I barked when Mom and Dad went out of the room. I didn't want them to leave me. So when this happened, they simply put me in the car with the windows open. I had plenty of fresh air and was comfortable there, and they could go relax and get something to eat, or run errands for a while.

I now have this Service Dog job down to a science, and I am almost perfect at it. In the airplanes, they now give us front row seats and I get to sleep at Mom and Dad's feet. By the time people are getting on the plane, they are surprised to see ME, an official Service Dog, sitting in the first row! Boy, am I hot stuff. I like it when everybody tells me how good I am, too. Luckily, I never did tinkle except for once in the airport terminal, when two little boys came over to see me. I really, really wanted to play with them…

See you later, everybody.

Love,

Mister Zippy

Bailey as a service dog, Avalon

Chapter Seven

St. Maarten Adventures

Hi again, everybody –

Dad likes to fix my wagon by taking me for a lot of long runs with him. Being a marathon runner, he gets us way out in the middle of nowhere and he practically has to drag me back home. I really get pooped sometimes. The swims on the beach are wonderful. We now take more "days off" to go to the beach, but as daughter Kelly always asks us, "Your days off from what?"

I am convinced that my favorite place to be in the entire world is floating neck-deep in the water at the south end of Orient Bay. My second place is in our pool, except that it is difficult to float for long because it is only fresh water, which doesn't have the buoyancy of salt water. That's where my raft comes in – I can float for hours! Mom 'n Dad will have friends come over for dinner on the terrace, and they spend the whole time laughing at me as I curl up and float forever. To me, this is even better than swimming. It's not as much work, and when I float, I can see over the pool wall and look at the ocean and the boat lights going by. Fun, man!

Mom 'n Dad 'n I noticed in St. Maarten that it is customary for the drivers of taxis, buses, cars, and vans to print slogans on their windshields. It makes the island quite colorful. Actually, it gives us a glimpse of who they are, and reminds us of how very religious the island-people can be. Here are a few, in no particular order: **Jesus Save,** Potato, Psalm 121, **Stainless Steel**, **Rising Star,** Sugar Lips, **Peaches**, **Taxi,** **First Class,** **Christ Capable,** Sweets, **VIP 2,** Sweet Rose of Sharon, **Bent, and Simplicity**. Our overall favorite is "*Praise is what I do*".

Hey, do you remember my encounter with the skunk? Well, I got sprayed three more times! Skunks are a little like a needle in a haystack, but I can sure find 'em. Dad still gets the skunk clean-up detail, but now he has it down to a science. Outside.

We still see Sparky in St. Maarten in the mornings, and we give him his blueberry. He smiles up at us and then scurries back into his little house between the rocks. I still like these little geckos. But now, I've discovered land crabs! We see them during our walks in the evening. They scurry across the road waving their arms, which is scary. It's like their arms have special weapons on the ends and they try to grab me with them. Dad calls these "pinchers". I especially like the flat ones that have been run over by a car. Boy, I can scoop these up in my mouth in no time and flip them in the air before Dad can catch me. It's a fun game I like to play.

One evening, we heard what sounded like a little animal building his house on top of our metal roof. It was quite annoying and we wondered what it was. So Dad got his ladder out and climbed up for a look. What a surprise to find a land crab was scurrying around on our roof, and in and out of the gutters! How in the world did he get there? I wondered about this for a long time until I finally discovered a land crab climbing UP the wall, sideways. So that's how they do it! When this guy saw me, his big arms flew out in front of him, weapons ready in case I advanced.

Folks, I saved you the best news for last. Mom got some great results on her PET Scans. After all the hard work of the last few months, the scans were clear! No cancer! This made us all very, very happy and we can really live again. The best part is, Mom now takes me for walks and I can still rest on the bed with her. I know she loves to cook and Dad says she really has the energy now to "go to town". But I don't understand why she would want to "go there", when I want her here with me!

We are staying here in Avalon for a couple more months and then we will go back to St. Maarten for Christmas. This year it will be special and the kids will come to visit – Kelly and Jim, Keira and Connor, and Lisa, Dave and Cole. Yay! It's great to have grandchildren in the house with us. We always have lots of fun. Oh, and the first thing I want to do when we get there is to see if Ducky has figured out how to swim! What do you think?

Meanwhile, I love you all!

Zippy

Overhead shot of Bailey in raft with Mom

Don, Bailey & Cindy in foyer

Made in the USA
Charleston, SC
15 August 2012